AGLIO

Garlic

Lovers

Cookbook

AGLIO

Garlic

Lovers

Cookbook

Caroline Sherman

Foreword by
Diane Merryman, Health & Wellness Coach

Arabelle Publishing
Chesterfield, VA

AGLIO: Garlic Lovers Cookbook
Copyright © 2019 by Caroline Sherman

ISBN (978-0-9979126-7-8)

Cover Design: Lance Buckley
Interior Illustrations: CanStock Photo

Published by Arabelle Publishing, LLC
PO Box 2841, Chesterfield, VA 23832
www.arabellepublishing.com
hello@arabellepublishing.com

Printed in the USA

"Garlic is divine. Few food items can taste so many distinct ways, handled correctly. Misuse of garlic is a crime. Old garlic, burnt garlic, garlic cut too long ago and garlic that has been tragically smashed through one of those abominations, the garlic press, are all disgusting. Please treat your garlic with respect. Sliver it for pasta, like you saw in Goodfellas; don't burn it. Smash it, with the flat of your knife blade if you like, but don't put it through a press. I don't know what that junk is that squeezes out the end of those things, but it ain't garlic. And try roasting garlic. It gets mellower and sweeter if you roast it whole, still on the clove, to be squeezed out later when it's soft and brown. Nothing will permeate your food more irrevocably and irreparably than burnt or rancid garlic. Avoid at all costs that vile spew you see rotting in oil in screw-top jars. Too lazy to peel fresh? You don't deserve to eat garlic." Anthony Bourdain, Kitchen Confidential

Table of Contents

Foreword

Garlic is one magical ingredient that makes your mouth water when cooking, makes your taste buds explode with excitement when you take a bite, and even creates lively conversation at the dinner table about its health benefits. But as I am cooking less and eating more raw foods, I am finding I often forget to add it in its original form until the dish is done, then I sprinkle garlic powder over the last few bites. Boy, I am missing out on the whole enjoyable garlic experience. Note to self, start cooking more with garlic!

In this cookbook, Caroline Sherman has embraced the power of garlic with her easy to prepare dishes that will keep you trying one right after the other. Savory or sweet, you are sure to find a favorite you will serve over and over again.

Garlic is a plant in the Allium family, a close relative to the lily flower. These little bulbs are related to onions, leeks, and shallots and have been around for centuries. What you may not realize is that they were first coveted for their health benefits and medicinal uses. The bulbs are made up of a cluster of cloves and often measured accordingly. One teaspoon equal about two cloves of chopped or minced garlic.

Garlic has been claimed to cure everything from the common cold to heart disease. Medical studies are inconclusive; however, some evidence shows improvement in lowering HDL cholesterol and blood pressure. Garlic may also improve digestion and has been identified by some researchers as antibacterial, antimicrobial, antifungal, and anti-parasitic. The recommended dosage for improved health is eating one to two cloves daily. In addition, garlic has very few calories and is nutritious. Just one clove contains all of this healthy goodness: vitamin C, vitamin B6, manganese, selenium, copper, calcium, phosphorus, potassium, iron, and Vitamin B1. Garlic has no fats or noticeable calories, so it is an excellent addition to a weight loss program, adding plenty of flavor without unwanted weight gain.

What most of us know best about garlic is the breath it leaves behind after lunch or dinner, or breakfast if you are adding it to an omelet or egg dish. When the cloves are cut, grated or smashed, they release an enzyme called alliinase. The enzyme produces a compound called allicin which creates an intense aroma and flavor. Allicin is produced as a line of defense to ward off worms or other animals from the plant. For the best enzyme impact, chop, or crush garlic and let sit for five to 10 minutes before cooking.

Garlic has four intensities, mild, medium, full, and intense flavor. Mild flavor comes from slicing the garlic. Peel the bulb, separate the cloves, and slice them from narrow tip to bottom. The flavor is increased by dicing the clove. Start by slicing then slice again crosswise creating tiny cubes. Mincing steps the flavor up a notch. Once the cloves are diced, scrape the pieces into a mound and cut them again with a sharp knife, creating very tiny pieces. Smashed cloves create the most intense flavor because it releases the juices and oils. This can be done with a large chef's knife laid sideways over the clove and hitting the blade firmly to smash it, or by laying the blade over the minced pieces and applying pressure by pressing on the blade and moving it in small circles over the pieces until the juices are evident.

There are three ways to use garlic to enhance the flavor of food. Raw garlic, whole or cut is often added to salad dressings and marinades. Sautéed garlic is when the cut cloves are heated in a pan with butter or cooking oil. Garlic burns quickly as does butter, so be careful not to overcook, or it may become bitter. Roasted garlic brings out the delicious flavor and full aroma. Remove the skins from the bulb but keep it intact. Cut about ¼ of an inch of the top. Place bulb on a sheet of aluminum foil and drizzle with cooking oil of your choice. Wrap tightly and cook in a preheated oven at 350 degrees for approximately two hours or until tender. There are plenty more recipes in these pages. From soup to sorbet, Caroline has you covered for any event whether you are dining alone or have a house full of guests.

Thank you, Caroline, for reminding me to re-explore this potent and flavorful ingredient. From now on, I will definitely add more garlic to my dishes.

Diane Merryman
Health & Wellness Coach

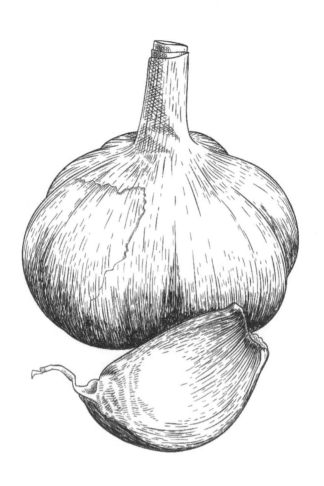

Marinades, Dressings & Dips

Simple Roasted Garlic

- 6 garlic heads
- 6 tablespoons extra-virgin olive oil

Preheat oven to 350 degrees. Using a sharp knife, cut a ½ inch off each garlic head. Arrange prepared garlic heads in a shallow glass baking dish and drizzle with olive oil. Bake 45 to 60 minutes or until soft, then brush with olive oil.

Fresh garlic becomes rich with a mellow flavor when roasted. Use in marinades, dressings, or dips.

Caramelized Garlic

- ½ cup sugar
- 6 tablespoons water
- ½ cup peeled garlic cloves
- 2 tablespoons butter, unsalted
- 1 tablespoon brandy

In a small heavy skillet, add sugar and moisten evenly with 2 tablespoons of water. Cook over medium heat, tipping the pan and gently swirling sugar mixture occasionally until sugar turns a golden color. Gradually add remaining water and mix well. Add garlic cloves, stir to coat and continue to heat 2 minutes. Stir in butter and brandy. Serve lukewarm.

Roasted Garlic Spread

- 1 head elephant garlic
- 3 cups cooked white beans
- ¼ teaspoon crushed red pepper flakes

Preheat oven to 300 degrees. Remove loose outer skin from garlic. In a shallow pan, place whole garlic heads, root end down and roast for 1 to 1 ¼ hours or until garlic is soft. Cool and squeeze softened garlic out of the skin. Mix the roasted garlic pulp with white beans in a food processor until smooth.

This is a delicious spread paired with toast points or crackers. Eliminate red pepper for a milder spread.

Garlic Seasoning Paste

- 18–24 large garlic cloves, peeled
- 2 tablespoons extra-virgin olive oil
- 2 tablespoons soy sauce
- 1 tablespoon honey
- dash Cayenne pepper

Combine all ingredients in a blender and process until smooth. Store in an air-tight container and refrigerate. Makes a ½ cup.

A savory grill seasoning for fish, chicken, ribs or hamburgers. Rub under turkey or chicken skin before roasting, or add to soups, salad dressings, and pasta.

Garlic Oil

- 1 head garlic
- 3 cups extra-virgin olive oil

Separate garlic into cloves and peel. Place in a jar or bottle. For a decorative effect, thread garlic cloves on a bamboo skewer. Fill the container with oil and seal tightly. Let stand overnight, then store in the refrigerator.

Flavored oils are expensive. Using this technique, you can develop your own unique blends at a fraction of the cost. Add fresh herbs, rosemary, or basil, and oregano.

Garlic Butter

- 4 cloves garlic, peeled
- 1 stick butter, softened
- salt

Boil water in a small pot and add garlic to blanch for about 2 minutes. Using a slotted spoon, remove garlic. Mince garlic in a food processor, blender, or spice grinder. Slice butter into tablespoon-size squares. Add butter and process until combined. Salt to taste and stir. Transfer softened butter to a small serving crock and refrigerate. Makes a ½ cup.

A flavorful spread for bread and crackers. Tuck a pat or two under chicken or turkey skin before roasting or melt over hot grilled fish or steak.

Garlic Mayonnaise

- 6 cloves of garlic
- ½ teaspoon of sea salt
- 1 ¼ cups mayonnaise

Crush garlic and salt together. In a small bowl, mix crushed garlic mixture and mayonnaise together until blended.

This makes a tasty spread for sandwiches. Add ketchup, and it becomes a delicious fry sauce. To mix, start with a small amount and gradually add ketchup until you reach the desired taste.

Garlic Parmesan Pesto

- 2 cups firmly packed fresh basil leaves
- ¾ cup grated Parmesan cheese
- ¾ cup extra-virgin olive oil
- 3 cloves garlic, peeled
- ¼ cup pine nuts

Place all ingredients into a blender or food processor. Cover and blend on medium speed for about 3 minutes, occasionally stopping to scrape the sides. Continue until smooth.

Pesto is one of the most versatile spreads. Use as a topping for sandwiches, meats, or vegetables. A delicious addition to soups or pasta.

Oil & Garlic Sauce

- ½ cup extra-virgin olive oil
- 4 cloves garlic, sliced thin
- 2 teaspoons lemon juice
- 2 tablespoons chopped herbs (basil, chives, oregano, savory, tarragon, parsley, or thyme.)
- ⅛ teaspoon black pepper

In a skillet, heat olive oil. Add sliced garlic and cook until browned. Slowly stir in lemon juice. Add parsley and pepper, and simmer for 10 minutes. Serve over hot cooked spaghetti.

Here are a few variations of this recipe, try adding one ingredient to the herbs: 5 chopped anchovy fillets, 2 tablespoons chopped walnuts, or 2 tablespoons capers.

Lemon Garlic Vinaigrette

- ¼ cup olive oil
- 1 tablespoon grated lemon peel
- 3 tablespoons lemon juice
- ½ teaspoon salt
- ¼ teaspoon fresh ground pepper
- 1 clove garlic, finely chopped

Mix all ingredients together.

Garlic Cream Cheese Dressing

- 1 (8-ounce) package cream cheese
- ½ cup sour cream
- ¼ cup milk
- 1 teaspoon lemon juice
- 2 garlic cloves, minced
- dash of salt and pepper

Combine ingredients until well blended. Chill. Serve with vegetables or salads. Makes about 1 ½ cups.

Creamy Garlic Dressing

- 1 cup mayonnaise
- 3 tablespoons whole milk
- 2 tablespoons cider vinegar
- 1 medium garlic clove, crushed
- ½ teaspoon sugar
- ¼ teaspoon salt
- pinch of pepper to taste

Stir ingredients together. Cover and chill.

Asian Garlic Marinade

- ¼ cup olive oil
- 4 cloves garlic, finely chopped
- 1 tablespoon rosemary leaves, chopped
- ½ teaspoon dry mustard
- 2 teaspoons soy sauce
- ¼ cup red or white vinegar
- ¼ cup dry sherry or apple juice

In a 10-inch skillet, heat oil over medium-high heat. Cook garlic in oil frequently stirring until golden. Stir in rosemary, mustard, and soy sauce, and remove from heat. Add vinegar and sherry and cool mixture.

May use 1 teaspoon dried rosemary in place of fresh. This marinade can be paired with beef, pork, or lamb. Pour over meat and refrigerate up to 24 hours for tasty, tender meat that will melt in your mouth!

Smoked Garlic Pepper Rub

- 1-2 tablespoons liquid smoke seasoning
- 1 teaspoon garlic powder
- 2 teaspoons cracked black pepper

Brush 4 to 5-pound bone-in beef, pork, or lamb roast with liquid smoke. Dust evenly with garlic powder and rub into meat. Sprinkle with pepper and press into meat. Cover and refrigerate meat at least 1 hour but not longer than 24 hours. Roast as desired.

GARLIC

Asian Garlic Ginger Rub

- 2 teaspoons ground ginger
- 3 garlic cloves, minced
- 2 teaspoons sea salt
- 1 teaspoon ground pepper
- 1 teaspoon red pepper flakes
- pinch Cayenne Pepper

Mix all ingredients together. Use the mixture to press on meats and poultry before cooking,

Spicy Garlic Salsa

- 10 garlic cloves, peeled and chopped
- ¾ cup fresh Italian parsley, chopped
- ½ cup olive oil
- salt and pepper to taste
- ¼ teaspoon dried red pepper flakes

In a small bowl, combine garlic, parsley, and olive oil. Season to taste with salt, pepper, and dried pepper flakes.

Garlic Lemon Hummus

- 2 (15-ounce) cans chickpeas
- 1 tablespoon Tahini
- juice from 2 lemons
- 3–4 cloves garlic
- ½ teaspoon salt (or more to taste)

Drain 1 can of chickpeas and add to a food processor. Add the second can undrained. Add remaining ingredients and puree until smooth.

Creamy Garlic & Herb Dip

- ½ cup low-fat cream cheese
- ¼ cup buttermilk
- 2 tablespoons fresh chives, minced
- 1 tablespoon fresh parsley, minced
- 1 teaspoon grated lemon rind
- ¼ teaspoon salt
- pinch freshly ground pepper (or more to taste)
- 1 small garlic clove, minced

In a medium bowl, combine all ingredients. Beat with an electric mixer at high speed for 2 minutes or until smooth.

Roasted Garlic Eggplant Dip

- 2 eggplants, ends trimmed
- garlic-infused olive oil
- salt, black pepper & cumin
- 4 garlic cloves, minced
- 2 tablespoons olive oil
- 2 tablespoons lemon juice
- fresh parsley, chopped

Preheat oven to 450 degrees. Cut eggplants in half lengthwise and score flat sides. Rub with garlic-infused olive oil and season tops with salt, pepper, and cumin. Bake until soft and charring about 1 hour. Set aside and cool. Scrape out eggplant pulp and coarsely chop. Place in a bowl and mix with garlic, olive oil, and lemon juice. Mash with a fork to a chunky consistency. Adjust seasonings to taste and sprinkle with fresh parsley for garnish. Makes about 2 cups.

Tuscan Garlic Bean Dip

- 2 (15-ounce) cans pinto beans
- 4 cloves garlic, minced
- 2 tablespoons olive oil
- 1 tablespoon soy sauce
- 1 tablespoon cider vinegar
- 1 teaspoon Cayenne pepper
- 1 (15-ounce) can of tomatoes, diced
- 1 small can green chilis, drained and chopped
- 1 small yellow onion, chopped
- 1 tablespoon fresh parsley, chopped

Place beans, garlic, olive oil, soy sauce, vinegar, parsley, and Cayenne pepper in a food processor and blend until smooth. Add tomatoes, green chilis, and chopped onion. Mix well. Pour into a serving bowl and garnish with fresh parsley. Serve with crackers, chips, toasted pita bread, or raw vegetables.

Garlic Cowboy Caviar

- 1 (15-ounce) can black beans, drained
- 1 (15-ounce) can yellow corn, drained
- 6 cloves garlic, crushed
- ½ cup chopped white onion
- ½ cup chopped red pepper
- ½ cup chopped green pepper
- 1 (4-ounce) can diced jalapeno peppers
- 1 (14.5-ounce) can diced tomatoes, drained
- 1 cup Greek salad dressing
- salt and pepper to taste
- chopped cilantro

In a medium bowl, combine all ingredients. Cover and refrigerate overnight to allow the flavors to blend. Serve with tortilla chips.

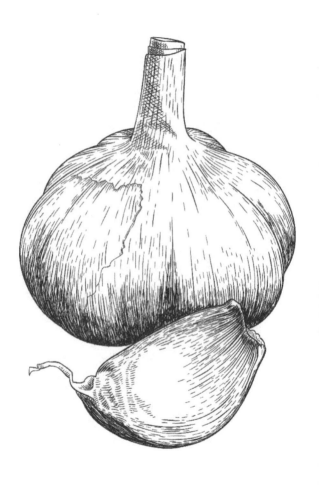

Salads & Appetizers

Garlic Three-Bean Salad

- ½ cup sugar
- ½ cup olive oil
- ½ cup balsamic vinegar
- 1 teaspoon garlic salt
- 2-4 cloves garlic, peeled & minced
- ½ cup chopped white onion
- 1 (16-ounce) can cut green beans, drained
- 1 (16-ounce) can cut wax beans, drained
- 1 (16-ounce) can red kidney beans, drained
- 6 tablespoons extra-virgin olive oil

Mix all ingredients in a medium bowl. Toss well. Cover and refrigerate overnight.

Spinach & Mushroom Salad & Garlic Dressing

- 8 ounces Applewood Smoked bacon
- ¾ cup olive oil
- ¼ cup red wine vinegar
- pinch salt & pepper
- 1 clove garlic, minced
- 1-pound leaf spinach, tough stems removed
- 8 ounces baby portabella mushrooms, thinly sliced

In a medium skillet, cook bacon over medium heat until crisp. Drain on paper towels and cool. Crumble and set aside. In a small bowl, whisk together oil, vinegar, salt, pepper, and garlic. Wash spinach leaves well and spin dry in a salad spinner. Tear leaves into small pieces and place in a medium salad bowl. Add mushrooms and bacon and toss to combine. Pour dressing over salad (refrigerate any leftovers). Toss salad and serve immediately.

Garlic & Mushrooms

- ¼ cup olive oil
- 3 tablespoons butter
- 10 baby portabella mushrooms, stems removed
- 2 green onions, chopped
- 2 teaspoons minced elephant garlic

In a skillet, heat oil and butter on low heat. Add mushrooms, chopped green onions, and garlic. Cook on low heat for 12-15 minutes until mushrooms are cooked. Remove mushrooms and enjoy. Makes 2 servings.

Elephant Garlic

Garlic Shrimp

- ½ cup butter, softened
- 2 tablespoons minced fresh parsley
- 1 heaping tablespoon minced shallots
- 4 cloves garlic, minced
- ¼ teaspoon paprika
- ⅛ teaspoon Cayenne pepper
- ⅛ teaspoon salt
- 2 teaspoons Pernod liquor
- ½ teaspoon lemon juice
- 1½ pounds shrimp, shelled and deveined
- flour
- olive oil
- juice of ½ lemon
- ¾ cup dry white wine

Cream butter with a wooden spoon. Add parsley, shallots, garlic and seasonings, Pernod and ½ teaspoon lemon juice; mix well and set aside. Coat shrimp with flour. Heat olive oil in a large skillet; shake flour from shrimp and sauté quickly, about 3 minutes until shrimp turn pink. Turn and continue to sauté another 3 minutes. Drain oil from skillet. Add ½ cup lemon juice and wine, and shake pan briefly overheat, about 1 minute. Add reserved garlic butter and toss shrimp quickly using a wooden spoon. Melt butter and serve immediately.

Hungarian Shrimp & Garlic

- ¼ cup extra-virgin olive oil
- 4 large garlic cloves, minced
- 1 teaspoon crushed red pepper flakes
- 1-pound jumbo shrimp, peeled and deveined
- 2 tablespoons dry sherry
- ½ teaspoon smoked paprika
- salt and pepper
- a generous handful of fresh flat-leaf parsley, finely chopped
- 1 lemon

In a large skillet, heat olive oil over medium heat. Add garlic and red pepper flakes and cook for 2 minutes. Raise temperature to high and add shrimp, sherry, and paprika. Cook, stirring until shrimp turns pink, about 3 minutes. Season with salt and pepper, parsley and lemon juice to taste. Makes 4 servings.

Garlic Smoked Salmon Squares

- 5 slices of sourdough bread
- 1 (3-ounce) package cream cheese, softened
- 3 ounces sliced smoked salmon
- 1 head roasted garlic (recipe page 7)
- Strips of peel cut from 2 large lemons

Toast bread slices and trim crusts. Spread softened cream cheese on each slice and cut into quarters. Spread roasted garlic pulp on each quarter, and top with a salmon slice. Garnish with lemon peel.

Elephant Garlic

Zucchini Cheese Garlic Squares

- 4 cups grated zucchini
- 1 ¾ cups biscuit baking mix
- ¾ cup grated Parmesan cheese
- 1 cup shredded sharp Cheddar cheese
- 4 eggs, beaten
- ⅔ cup vegetable oil
- 1 large finely chopped yellow onion
- 4 cloves chopped garlic
- 3 tablespoons dried parsley
- ½ teaspoons salt
- ¾ teaspoon dried oregano

Preheat oven to 400 degrees. In a mixing bowl, combine the zucchini, biscuit mix and remaining ingredients. Mix until blended. Spread into a greased 9 x 13-inch baking pan. Bake 25-30 minutes, until golden brown. Allow the mixture to cool. Cut into small squares and serve warm or cold.

Garlic Cheese Crisps

- 1 cup all-purpose flour
- 2 teaspoons garlic salt
- ⅓ cup butter, chilled
- 1 cup coarsely grated sharp Cheddar cheese
- 1 tablespoon Worcestershire sauce
- 1-2 teaspoons ice water (optional)

Preheat oven to 400 degrees. Mix flour and garlic salt in a small bowl and cut in butter with a knife or pastry blender until mixture resembles coarse meal; add cheese and toss well. Sprinkle Worcestershire sauce over the mixture and stir lightly with a fork. Ingredients should just hold together; if not, add ice water. Shape into ¾ inch balls and arrange 2 inches apart on ungreased baking sheets. Flatten each to ¼ inch thick. Bake 10–15 minutes until golden.

Garlic Cheese Ball

- ½ pound sharp Cheddar cheese, grated fine
- 1 (8-ounce) package cream cheese, softened to room temperature
- 2 cloves garlic, peeled and crushed
- pinch of salt
- ⅓ cup minced pecans or walnuts

Using your hands, mix cheeses, garlic, and salt until thoroughly blended, then shape into a ball. Roll the ball into minced nuts.

Honey Garlic Chicken Bites

- ½ cup Orange Blossom honey
- 2 tablespoons soy sauce
- 2 tablespoons balsamic vinegar
- ½ teaspoon ginger
- 3 cloves garlic, minced
- 1 tablespoon cornstarch
- 2 chicken breasts cut into 1-inch cubes

Mix ingredients together until well combined. Add chicken cubes and marinate for at least 2 hours or overnight. Place bites on a foil-lined baking tray. Bake in a preheated 400-degree oven.

Make an extra batch of honey soy mixture to use as a dip for cooked chicken bites. These chicken bites are also a tasty addition to salads and pasta dishes.

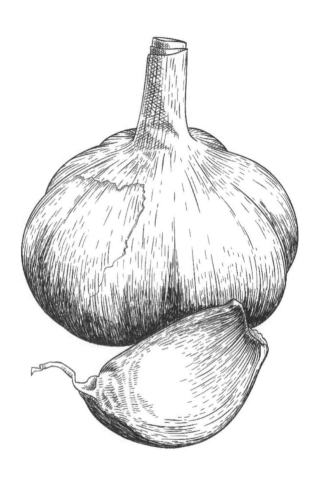

Breads

Garlicky Cheese Biscuits

- 2 cups baking mix
- ⅔ cup milk
- ½ cup shredded Smoked Cheddar
- 2 cloves garlic, minced
- ¼ stick butter, melted
- ¼ teaspoon garlic powder

Heat oven to 450 degrees. Mix baking mix, milk, cheese, and minced garlic to make a soft dough. Beat vigorously for 30 seconds. Drop 10–12 spoonsful of dough onto ungreased cookie sheet. Bake 8-10 minutes or until golden brown. Mix margarine and garlic powder; brush on warm biscuits before removing from cookie sheet. Serve warm.

Garlic Cheese Casserole Bread

- 2 tablespoons sugar
- 2 teaspoons sea salt
- 2 packages active dry yeast
- 5 cups flour
- 2 ¼ cups whole milk
- 1 cup shredded sharp Cheddar cheese
- 4 cloves garlic, peeled and minced
- 1 tablespoon butter

In a large bowl, combine dry ingredients, keeping 3 cups flour in reserve. In a small saucepan, heat milk, cheese, and garlic until very warm but not hot.

Beat liquid ingredients into the dry mixture until just blended. Add remaining flour one cup at a time until batter becomes a stiff dough. Cover with a towel and let rise in a warm place for about 45 minutes.

Punch down and turn into a greased 2-quart casserole dish. Cover and let rise until double, about 45 minutes. Preheat oven to 375 degrees. Brush loaf with melted butter. Bake 30-35 minutes until golden brown.

Garlic Veggie Garbage Bread

- 2 tablespoons extra-virgin olive oil
- 3 cloves garlic, minced
- 1 medium yellow squash
- 1 medium zucchini
- 2 medium Roma tomatoes
- 1 Vidalia onion
- 1 teaspoon oregano
- salt and pepper
- 1-pound pizza dough
- 8-10 thin slices mozzarella cheese
- 1 egg, whisked

Preheat oven to 375 degrees. Heat the olive oil in a skillet over medium heat. Add minced garlic and cook for a few minutes. Cut squash and zucchini in half lengthwise, and into thin slices and set aside. Thinly dice tomatoes and onion. Increase heat to medium-high and sauté onions with garlic until translucent. Add squash and zucchini and sauté until crisp-tender. Add tomatoes and sauté until they break down about 3-4 minutes. Add oregano, salt, and pepper, and sauté 2 minutes.

Roll pizza dough on a flat surface, making a rectangle approximately 11 x 17 inches. Lay mozzarella cheese on top, overlapping slices. Spoon vegetable mixture over cheese and roll the pizza dough like a burrito. Seal the end with whisked egg. Brush entire loaf with remaining egg. Place the roll on a baking sheet and bake until dough is cooked through and the crust is firm and lightly browned, about 40-45 minutes. Cut bread into 2-inch slices and serve warm.

Traditional Garlic Bread

- ⅓ cup stick butter, softened
- 1 clove garlic, finely chopped
- 1 loaf French bread, cut into 1-inch slices

Preheat oven to 400 degrees. Mix margarine and garlic; butter top of each bread slice. Reassemble loaf and wrap securely in heavy-duty aluminum foil. Bake 15-20 minutes or until hot.

GARLIC

Garlic Bruschetta

- thick crust Italian bread cut into 4 slices
- ½ cup extra-virgin olive oil
- 5-6 large cloves garlic
- sea salt
- cracked black pepper

Peel and slice garlic. Heat olive oil in a sauté pan and add garlic, cooking until garlic sizzles. Broil bread slices until toasty and golden brown. Brush olive oil on bread slices and top with garlic slices. Salt and pepper to taste.

Garlic Ham & Cheese Biscuits

- 1 ½ cups chopped ham
- 6 cloves of garlic, crushed
- 2 cups flour
- 2 teaspoons baking powder
- 1 cup (4 ounces) shredded extra-sharp cheddar cheese
- dash of Cayenne pepper
- 1 cup low-fat milk

In a medium skillet, sauté ham and garlic 3 minutes. In a medium bowl, combine ham mixture, flour, baking powder, cheese, and red pepper. Add milk, stirring until just moistened. Spray baking sheet with cooking spray. Drop batter by heaping tablespoons onto a baking sheet. Bake in a preheated oven at 400 degrees for 20 minutes or until lightly browned.

Easy Peasy Garlic Knots

- ¼ cup butter, melted
- 4 tablespoons grated Parmesan cheese
- 3 garlic cloves, minced
- ½ teaspoon dried oregano
- ½ teaspoon dried parsley
- ¼ teaspoon of sea salt
- 1 (16-ounce) tube refrigerated buttermilk biscuits

Preheat oven to 400 degrees. Lightly coat a baking sheet with cooking spray. In a small bowl, mix all ingredients and set aside. Roll each biscuit into a long rope. Cut in half and tie each piece into a knot. Roll each knot into the butter mixture and place on a cooking sheet. Brush knots with remaining butter mixture. Bake 8-10 minutes or until golden brown. Serve warm.

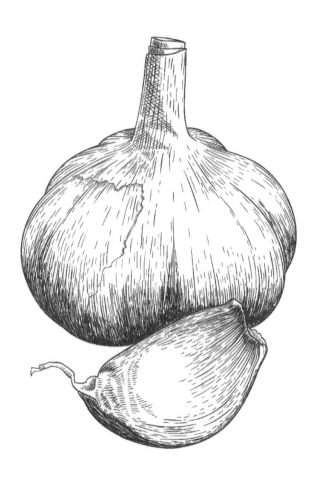

Soups

Roasted Cauliflower & Garlic Soup

- 1 large head cauliflower (2 ½ pounds)
- 4 ½ teaspoons olive oil
- 1 ½ teaspoons kosher salt, divided
- 3 cup reduced-sodium chicken stock
- 1 cup 2% reduced-fat milk
- ½ cup grated Parmesan cheese
- freshly ground pepper to taste
- fresh thyme leaves, for garnish
- pomegranate seeds, for garnish

Preheat oven to 425 degrees. Cut cauliflower into 2-inch florets; toss with olive oil and ½ teaspoon salt. Arrange florets in a single layer on a jelly roll pan or cookie sheet. Wrap garlic cloves in aluminum foil and place on the pan with florets. Bake 30-40 minutes, tossing every 15 minutes until cauliflower is golden brown.

Transfer cauliflower to a large Dutch oven. Unwrap garlic and cool for 5 minutes before adding to Dutch oven. Add stock and bring to a simmer over medium heat. Simmer, occasionally stirring, for 5 minutes. Let mixture cool 10 minutes. Process cauliflower mixture in a blender (small batches) until smooth, scraping down sides as needed. Return blended mixture to Dutch oven. Stir in milk, cheese, and remaining teaspoon of salt. Cook over low heat, occasionally stirring, 2 to 3 minutes until heated. Add pepper to taste. Add thyme leaves and pomegranate seeds for garnish.

Mexicana Garlic Soup

- 4 tablespoons butter
- 8 cloves garlic, crushed
- 2 tablespoons flour
- 1 ½ quarts chicken stock
- 2 drops Tabasco sauce
- ¼ teaspoon pepper
- 6 eggs
- 4 tablespoons chopped leaf parsley
- ¼ cup crumbled corn chips

In a large, heavy saucepan, melt butter over medium heat. Stir in garlic and flour until the garlic is tender, and the flour is absorbed. Stir in stock and bring to a boil. Reduce heat and simmer, covered for 10 minutes. Add Tabasco sauce and seasonings. Slide eggs into soup and poach. Ladle soup into bowls with one egg in each serving dish. Sprinkle with parsley and crumbled chips.

Garbanzo Garlic Soup

- 2 teaspoons olive oil
- 1 clove garlic, minced
- 1 cup yellow onion, finely chopped
- 2 cups fresh spinach, washed, drained and chopped
- 1 (8-ounce) can garbanzo beans, rinsed and drained
- 4 plum tomatoes, peeled, seeded, and diced
- 1 ½ quarts water
- 1 ½ ounces uncooked orzo pasta
- 2 teaspoons fresh parsley, chopped

In a medium skillet, heat oil. Add garlic and onions, cooking over medium-high heat stirring often. Add spinach and cook 1 to 2 minutes, stirring, until spinach is wilted. Add garbanzo beans and tomatoes, and 1 ½ quarts water and bring to a boil. Stir in pasta and let simmer until pasta is tender. Sprinkle with fresh parsley.

Garlic Squash Soup

- 1 small butternut squash
- 2 cloves garlic, minced
- ½ cup yellow onion, chopped
- ½ head cauliflower, chopped
- 4 cups of water
- ½ cup rolled oats
- ¼ teaspoon lemon juice
- ⅛ teaspoon lime juice

In a heavy saucepan, combine all ingredients and bring to a boil. Reduce heat and simmer for 30 minutes. Puree in a blender and serve warm.

Garlic Chicken Bone Broth

- ¼ cup extra-virgin olive oil
- 2 heads of garlic, peeled and mashed
- 4 cups of chicken bone broth
- salt and pepper to taste

In a small Dutch oven, add olive oil and smashed garlic and cook over medium heat. Do not let the garlic get brown. Add bone broth and bring to a boil, then reduce heat and simmer for 15 minutes.

Asian Garlic Health Soup

- 4 heads of roasted garlic, squeeze out pulp (recipe on page 7)
- 4 tablespoons butter
- 2-3 scallions, chopped
- 2 teaspoons fresh chopped thyme
- 1 teaspoon dried oregano
- 3 teaspoons fresh Thai basil
- ½ teaspoon of sea salt
- ½ teaspoon black pepper
- 4 cups of chicken bone broth
- 2 cups of coconut milk

In a Dutch oven, sauté roasted garlic pulp, scallions, and spices in butter. Add chicken bone broth and simmer for 15-20 minutes. Add coconut milk and reduce heat. Blend soup with a wire whisk or immersion blender

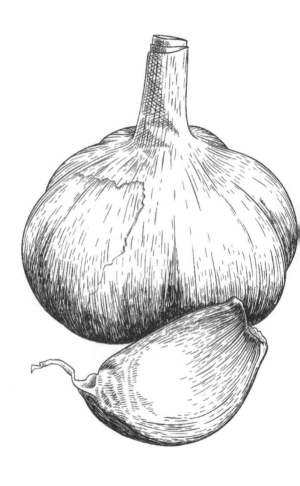

Sides

Roasted Garlic Potatoes

- 3 large baking potatoes, quartered
- 1 tablespoon minced garlic
- 2 teaspoons chopped fresh rosemary
- 2 tablespoons olive oil
- coarse sea salt and freshly ground pepper

Preheat oven to 350 degrees. Cut each potato quarter into wedges and arrange in a greased shallow baking dish. Combine garlic, rosemary and olive oil, and brush over potatoes. Season with salt and pepper to taste. Bake 45 minutes to 1 hour, turning several times.

Russet Garlic Potatoes

- 1 ½ pounds russet potatoes
- 2 garlic cloves, minced
- 2 tablespoons olive oil
- 1 teaspoons salt
- ½ teaspoon cracked black pepper

Preheat oven to 450 degrees. Cut potatoes in 1-inch pieces. In a 9x13 inch roasting pan, toss potatoes with remaining ingredients. Roast 20 minutes or until tender, stirring once. Place under broiler for extra crispiness.

GARLIC

Garlic Basil Tomatoes

- 4 medium tomatoes, cut into ¼-inch slices
- ¼ cup olive oil
- 1 tablespoon chopped fresh basil leaves
- 2 tablespoons red wine vinegar
- ⅛ teaspoon salt
- 3 drops red pepper sauce
- 2 cloves garlic, finely chopped
- salad greens, optional

Place tomatoes in a glass dish. Shake remaining ingredients together in a tightly covered container. Pour over tomatoes. Cover and refrigerate at least 3 hours to blend flavors, turn occasionally. Serve on top of salad greens.

Garlic Asparagus

- 1 (14-ounce) can reduced-sodium chicken broth
- 3 tablespoons olive oil
- 12 garlic cloves, peeled and cut in halves lengthwise
- 1 ½ pound asparagus, trimmed
- coarse sea salt and freshly ground pepper
- Grated rind of 1 lemon

In a large skillet, bring broth, oil, and garlic to a boil. Add asparagus and return to a boil. Reduce heat to medium, cover and cook until asparagus is tender but still crisp about 5 minutes. With a slotted spoon, transfer asparagus to a warm serving plate. Raise heat and melt remaining liquid until syrupy and reduced to about ½ cup. Season with salt and pepper to taste. Pour over asparagus and sprinkle with grated lemon rind.

Asian Green Beans

- 1 tablespoon peanut or sesame oil
- 2 cloves garlic, thinly sliced
- 1-pound fresh green beans, trimmed
- 1 tablespoon white sugar
- 2 tablespoons oyster sauce
- 2 tablespoons soy sauce

Heat oil in a wok or large skillet over medium heat. Stir in garlic and cook until edges brown, about 20 seconds. Add green beans and keep stirring, cooking until beans soften about 5 minutes. Stir in sugar, oyster sauce, and soy sauce. Continue stir-frying for several minutes until the beans are tender.

Zesty Garlic Lima Beans

- 1 (10-ounce) package frozen baby lima beans, cooked and cooled
- ½ cup thinly sliced red peppers
- 3 cloves garlic, minced
- ¼ cup Italian dressing
- 1 teaspoon fresh herbs

Mixed drained lima beans with remaining ingredients. Combine well and refrigerate to chill and allow flavors to blend.

Garlic Mashed Cauliflower

- 1 large head of cauliflower
- 5 cloves of garlic
- 2 tablespoons butter
- ¼ teaspoon freshly ground nutmeg
- Sea salt and ground pepper to taste

In a large 6-quart steamer add water to about 2 inches deep and heat to boiling. Meanwhile, wash and separate cauliflower into small pieces. Mince garlic cloves in a garlic press. Add cauliflower and garlic to the pot and cook for about 10-15 minutes or until soft. Mash together and add butter and season with nutmeg, and salt and pepper to taste.

Mashed cauliflower is an excellent alternative to potatoes for those looking to cut calories or lower glycemic index.

Garlic and Herb Spinach Cakes

- 1 tablespoon olive oil
- 2 pounds fresh spinach, chopped
- 2 tablespoons of minced garlic
- 1 teaspoon fresh rosemary, minced
- 4-5 small new white potatoes
- 2 eggs
- ½ cup seasoned breadcrumbs
- additional breadcrumbs for coating
- 4 ounces grated Parmesan cheese

In a medium skillet, heat olive oil and cook spinach and garlic. Remove spinach and set aside. Boil potatoes until soft. Mash and let cool. Beat eggs and mix all ingredients together. Form into 3-inch cakes and roll in breadcrumbs. Return cakes to skillet and brown over medium heat. Place browned cakes on a cookie sheet and bake in a 375-degree oven for 20 minutes.

Garlic Spiced Carrots

- 1 ½ pounds carrots cut in ¼-inch slices
- 1 cup cranberries
- ½ cup butter
- ⅓ cup finely chopped yellow onion
- 2 cloves garlic, peeled and minced
- 2 teaspoons ground cinnamon
- 1 ½ teaspoons salt
- ¼ cup packed dark brown sugar

In a covered saucepan over low heat, cook carrots, cranberries, butter, onion, garlic, and spices until carrots are tender when pierced with a fork. Stir the mixture occasionally. Add brown sugar and cook until sugar is dissolved.

Simple Garlic Roasted Carrots

- 1 ½ pounds carrots, peeled and cut into chunks
- 3 tablespoons butter
- 6 cloves garlic, minced
- ¼ teaspoon Himalayan salt
- ¼ teaspoon fresh ground pepper
- Chopped Italian parsley

Preheat oven to 425 degrees. Prepare a baking sheet and set aside. Cut up carrots. In a heavy skillet, melt butter and sauté garlic and spices until garlic is just softened. Do not overcook garlic as it will be bitter. Add carrots and toss until well combined. Arrange carrots on baking sheet in a single layer. Bake for 25-30 minutes. Garnish with chopped parsley.

You can vary this recipe by adding brussels sprouts.

Sautéed Celery with Garlic

- 2 tablespoons olive oil
- 1 small bunch celery cleaned and cut into diagonal slices
- 1 bunch green onions, chopped into 2- inch pieces
- 3 cloves garlic, sliced thin
- 2 bay leaves
- 1 teaspoon thyme leaves
- ¾ teaspoon salt
- ¼ teaspoon pepper

In a 4-quart saucepan, over medium heat, add oil, celery, green onions, garlic, and spices cook for about 5 minutes until the celery is tender-crisp. Discard bay leaves and serve hot.

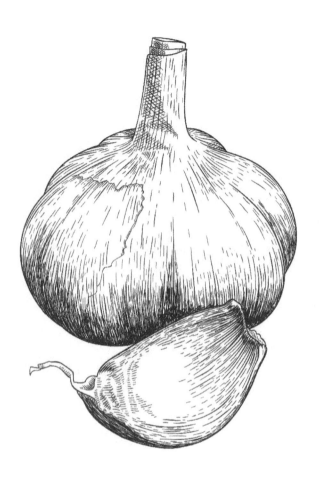

Entrees

Hungarian Roasted Chicken

- 1 whole chicken [about 3 pounds]
- ¼ cup butter, melted
- 6 cloves garlic, minced
- 1 ½ teaspoons onion powder
- ¼ teaspoon Hungarian Paprika
- ½ cup chicken stock
- ½ cup apple cider

Preheat oven to 350 degrees. Place chicken in a roasting pan and pour melted butter over the top. Sprinkle with minced garlic, onion powder, paprika, and a generous amount of salt and pepper. Pour chicken broth and apple cider into the bottom of the pan. Bake for 1 hour and 45 minutes, basting occasionally. Let rest 10 minutes before carving. Served drizzled with pan juices.

Herb Garlic Chicken Breasts

- 4 boneless, skinless chicken breasts
- 4 garlic cloves, minced
- 4 tablespoons brown sugar
- 1 tablespoon olive oil
- selection of fresh chopped herbs
- salt and pepper to taste

Preheat oven to 450 degrees. Line a baking dish with aluminum foil and lightly coat with cooking spray. In a small frying pan, sauté garlic in oil until tender. Remove from heat and stir in brown sugar. Add fresh chopped herbs, mix and set aside. Season chicken pieces with salt and pepper. Place breasts in a baking dish and smother with garlic sauce mixture. Bake uncovered for 15-30 minutes, or until juices run clear.

Garlic Basil Chicken Thighs

- 4 cloves garlic, minced
- 2 tablespoons fresh Thai basil leaves
- ½ teaspoon pepper
- ¼ teaspoon salt
- 1 tablespoon fresh lemon juice
- 2 tablespoons extra-virgin olive oil
- 1 ¼ pounds chicken thighs

Mix all ingredients. Coat each chicken thigh in garlic mixture. In a heavy skillet, add a little olive oil and lightly coat the pan. Cook chicken about 5 minutes on each side. Cover and cook 10-15 minutes longer until chicken is done. Juices will flow clear.

Garlic Scallop Kabobs

- 36 sea scallops
- 1 package country style bacon (divide into 36 strips)
- cooking spray
- 3 cloves garlic, minced
- ¼ cup lemon juice
- 2 tablespoons fresh Italian parsley
- ¾ teaspoons minced fresh oregano

Wrap each scallop with a strip of bacon. Thread 6 scallops onto 6 (12-inch) skewers and set aside. Heat a medium skillet and sauté garlic until browned. Remove from heat and stir in lemon juice, parsley, and oregano. Baste scallop skewers with lemon garlic mixture. Grill kabobs for about 9 minutes. Or bake in a 400-degree oven

Sweet Garlic Lamb Chops

- 4 (4-ounce) Lamb Chops
- olive oil
- ½ cup water
- ½ cup Marsala wine
- 2 tablespoons tomato paste
- 3 garlic cloves, minced
- 1 cup baby portabella mushrooms
- ¼ cup chopped yellow onion

Coat a large skillet with olive oil. Heat a skillet and add chops, cooking 7 minutes on each side. Remove chops from skillet. In a bowl, combine water, wine, tomato paste, and garlic; whisk together until well blended. Add wine mixture, mushrooms and onion to skillet and cook on high about two minutes. Add lamb chops back to pan and simmer for 5 minutes. Serve chops topped with mushroom and wine mixture.

Pork Roast with Garlic Sage

- 2 tablespoons minced garlic
- 1 tablespoon Himalayan Pink Salt
- 1 teaspoon ground pepper
- 1 tablespoon olive oil
- 1 (2 ¼ to 3 pounds) boneless pork loin roast
- whole fresh sage leaves

Preheat oven to 350 degrees. In a small bowl, combine garlic, salt, pepper and olive oil. Untie roast and unroll or separate pieces. With a sharp knife, make two or three half-inch deep slits along the length of the roast. Spread all but 2 teaspoons of garlic mixture over surface of meat, pressing into the slits. Cover with a layer of sage leaves. Roll and tie roast. Rub outside with remaining garlic mixture. Place in a roasting pan and roast 1 ¼ to 1 ½ hours, basting several times with drippings. Remove from oven and allow to stand 10 minutes. Slice about ½ inch thick.

Apricot Garlic Alaskan Salmon

- ⅓ cup apricot jelly or jam
- 3 cloves garlic, minced
- 1 ½ teaspoons cider vinegar
- ½ teaspoon lemon juice
- 4 (6-ounce) Alaskan salmon steaks

Mix apricot jelly, garlic, lemon juice and vinegar in a small bowl. Rinse and dry fish. Place fish in an oiled shallow glass baking dish. Spoon the apricot jelly mixture evenly on the salmon. Bake at 350 degrees for about 15 minutes or until the center of fish is opaque.

Garlic Pasta Alfredo

- 1 tablespoon butter
- 3 cloves garlic, minced
- 1 tablespoon flour
- 1 ⅓ cups whole milk
- 2 tablespoons cream cheese
- 1¼ cups freshly grated Parmesan cheese, divided
- 2 teaspoons chopped fresh parsley
- freshly ground pepper
- 4 cups hot cooked fettuccine

Melt butter in a saucepan over medium heat. Add garlic and sauté 1 minute. Stir in flour, and gradually add milk, stirring with a wire whisk until blended. Cook, stirring constantly, 5-10 minutes or until mixture is thick and bubbly. Stir in cream cheese and cook 2 minutes. Add 1 cup of Parmesan cheese, parsley, and pepper, stirring constantly until cheeses melt. Pour sauce over hot pasta and toss well to coat. Sprinkle with remaining Parmesan cheese.

Linguine with Garlic Pepper Oil

- 3 tablespoons extra-virgin olive oil
- ½ teaspoon dried crushed red pepper
- 6 cloves garlic, minced
- 6 cups hot cooked linguine
- ½ cup chopped fresh Italian parsley
- 1 teaspoon of sea salt
- ½ teaspoon pepper

Heat oil in a nonstick skillet over medium-high heat. Add red pepper; cook 2 minutes. Add garlic; sauté until garlic is lightly browned. Remove from heat; stir in pasta and remaining ingredients.

GARLIC

Garlic Lovers Mostaccioli

- 2 tablespoons fresh basil
- ¼ teaspoon salt
- ¼ teaspoon pepper
- 4-6 cloves garlic, minced
- 2 ¼ cups cooked Mostaccioli pasta
- 1 cup sliced baby portabella mushrooms
- ¾ cup cherry tomatoes, cut in half
- ½ cup chopped red pepper
- 1 cup shredded mozzarella cheese
- 1 cup grated Parmesan cheese

Heat a skillet with a little olive oil and combine all ingredients except pasta and cheese. Cook until garlic is lightly golden, and peppers are soft. Turn mixture into a greased baking dish and toss with pasta and cheese. Top with grated Parmesan cheese. Bake in a 400-degree oven until cheese is bubbly and lightly browned.

Garlic Turkey Burgers

- 2 pounds ground turkey meat
- 3 heads roasted garlic pulp
- salt and pepper to taste
- ½ cup breadcrumbs
- 1 large egg, lightly beaten
- 1 teaspoon chopped fresh basil
- 1 teaspoon chopped fresh thyme
- 1 teaspoon Worcestershire sauce

Combine all ingredients, mixing well with clean hands. Form into patties using about ½ cup meat. Grill burgers or cook in a preheated oven set at 350 degrees. Cook for about 20 minutes turning once.

Meat can be made ahead and used for burgers, meatballs, or tacos.

Indian Grilled Lamb

- juice and grated rind of one lemon
- ¼ cup olive oil
- ½ cup small onion, minced
- 8 garlic cloves, peeled and minced
- 3 tablespoons chopped fresh oregano
- 1 5-pound leg of lamb, butterflied
- sea salt
- Garlic Raita (page 81)

In a large, shallow dish, combine lemon juice and rind, olive oil, onion, garlic, and oregano. Add lamb and turn to coat on all sides. Cover and refrigerate overnight, turning several times. Grill over hot coals for about 40 minutes, turning and basting with marinade until cooked as desired. Cut into thin slices and serve with Garlic Raita.

Burani Garlic Raita

- 1 (6-ounce) container of plain yogurt
- ¼ cup sour cream
- 6 cloves garlic, minced
- 2 tablespoons chopped mint
- ½ teaspoon salt

Mix ingredients in a small bowl. Serve chilled.

Raita is a popular condiment in India which is a delicious accompaniment to meats, salads and can be a dip. If you prefer the taste of roasted garlic, this dish can be prepared with roasted garlic on page 7.

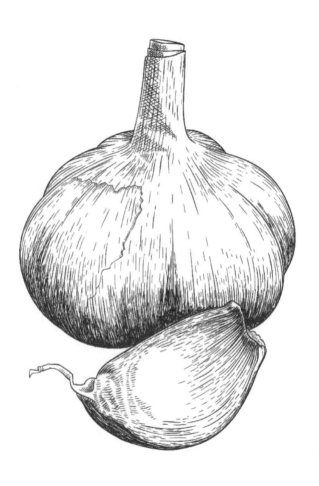

Desserts

Garlicky Lemon Sorbet

- 1 cup sugar
- 1 head roasted garlic, peeled
- the rind of one lemon
- dash of salt
- 3 cups of water
- ⅔ cups lemon juice

In a food processor, combine sugar, roasted garlic, lemon rind, and salt. Combine until lemon peel is finely chopped. Transfer to a saucepan and add water. Heat until sugar is dissolved. Let cool before adding lemon juice. Cover and chill. Process mixture in an ice cream maker according to the manufacturer's instructions. Scoop into small dishes or store tightly covered in freezer. Makes about one quart.

Garlic Vanilla Ice Cream

- 3 cups whole milk
- ½ tablespoon chopped garlic
- 1 cup heavy cream
- 1 ½ cups sugar
- 9 separated egg yolks
- 1 split vanilla pod

Pour milk into a saucepan and add garlic and vanilla. Bring to a boil, then remove from heat to cool. In a medium bowl, mix cream, sugar and egg yolks. Strain the milk and add to cream mixture, stirring constantly. Pour the combined mixture back to the saucepan and heat over medium heat to thicken, stirring constantly. When mixture is thick and coats the back of a spoon, let cook 10-15 minutes before cooling in an ice bath. Freeze overnight for 24 hours before serving.

Garlic French Bread Pudding

- 2 cups whole milk
- 8 cloves garlic, chopped
- 2 large eggs
- 1 cup sugar
- 2 separated egg yolks
- handful fresh parsley
- ¾ tablespoon salt
- 2 ½ cups ½-inch cubed French bread

Scald milk in a medium skillet. Turn off heat and add chopped garlic to infuse flavor into the liquid. Strain milk and slowly add to eggs and sugar, mixing well with a whisk. Add parsley and salt and pepper to taste. Divide bread cubes into muffin tin cups. Equally ladle egg mixture over the bread. Bake for 45 minutes until golden brown. Cool for 10 minutes before serving.

Garlicky Pineapple Cake

- ⅔ cup melted butter
- 1 cup packed light brown sugar
- 1 (20-ounce) can sliced pineapple, drained
- 10 cloves garlic, peeled
- 1 (18 ½ ounce) yellow cake mix

Preheat oven to 350 degrees. Spread butter over bottom of 9 a 13-inch baking dish. Sprinkle brown sugar evenly. Next, arrange a single layer of pineapple rings. In the center of each ring place 1 clove garlic. Prepare cake batter according to package directions. Pour mixture into prepared pan on top of pineapple slices. Bake 30-35 minutes, or until a cake tester inserted near center comes out clean. Cool on rack for 10 minutes. Loosen edges, then turn out onto a serving platter. Serve warm or at room temperature.

Black Garlic Truffles

- 1 (12-ounce) package dark chocolate pieces
- ¾ cup sweetened condensed milk
- 1 teaspoon vanilla extract
- ⅛ teaspoon salt
- 3 cloves black garlic, chopped
- ½ cup cocoa for garnish

In a 2-quart saucepan over low heat, melt chocolate pieces. Stir in condensed milk, vanilla, salt, and garlic until well mixed. Refrigerate mixture for 45 minutes until it is easy to shape. With buttered hands, shape mixture into 1-inch balls. Roll balls in cocoa.

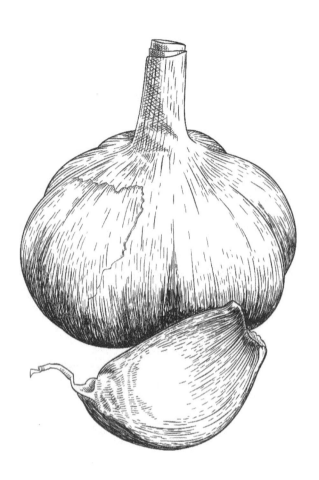

Cooking with Garlic

Garlic is one great flavor that can enhance almost any meat, vegetable, or pasta dish. The powder can be added to a savory rub for grilling or smoking meat. The cloves are flavorful when added to a sautéed vegetable dish. Minced garlic or garlic powder makes for a delicious addition to a cheese or tomato-based pasta sauce. Garlic cooks quickly in a pan with oil or butter, so add it at the end of the cooking time in a dish of sautéed vegetables. Powdered garlic, like most other spices, should be added at the end of the cooking time too to keep its flavor. Most spices lose their flavor if added at the beginning of the heating process.

With so many garlic varieties, how do you decide which to use? And did you know there are two types: softneck and hardneck?

The softneck variety may have up to 20 cloves, no center stem or flower and thick skins which are hard to peel. The thick skins give it a longer shelf life of up to eight months if kept in a cool dark place. The hardneck type usually have fewer cloves and a woody center stem that grows beyond the cloves with a flowering head. Its softer skins are easier to peel, but a shorter shelf life of only four of five months. Both types have multiple varieties, but the hardneck varieties usually have the most intense flavor. So, if you are seeking a more robust garlicky taste, look for a hardneck variety. (1)

You may have heard of elephant garlic too, but this type is a member of the onion family. The bulbs are larger with only a few cloves, and the flavor is more of a mild garlic/onion blend. With each type, the most intense flavor comes when the garlic bulb is cut, and the juices are released.

One of the easiest ways to peel garlic is to take a single clove and place it between your thumb and forefinger of each hand, then twist the clove with your thumbs and forefingers moving in opposite directions. This action breaks the skin and makes it easy to remove.

Typically, the scent will linger on your skin after it comes in contact with the cut garlic. There are three ways to effectively remove the smell. 1) Try rubbing your hands with a stainless-steel spoon under cold water. Use the spoon as if it was a bar of soap. 2) Rubbing your hands with a few coffee beans or a handful of coffee grounds has been reported to do the trick. 3) The third method is to rub your hands with a cut lemon; however, be careful with this technique if you have sensitive skin, or a cut or open wound. It will most likely sting–big time!!

There are at least five ways to prepare garlic for cooking: sliced, sliced/cross-sliced, minced, crushed, and grated. The flavor of garlic is released when the clove is cut, and the oils are released. The cut garlic can be soaked in water for the basis of an herbal tea, by itself or with additional herbs added. It can also be used with olive oil in salad dressings and marinades or cooked with butter or cooking oil. Garlic can also be added to softened butter as a paste and spread on bread or toast.

So whichever methods you choose for cutting and cooking, I hope you will use it more often and enjoy the robust flavor of garlic!

My Recipes

_____

_____

_____

_____

_____

_____

_____

_____

_____

_____

_____

Reference

(1) https://www.gardeningknowhow.com/edible/herbs/garlic/different-types-of-garlic.htm

Cookbooks from
Arabelle Publishing
Available on Amazon